What People Are Saying About

"Pizza Day – We Rise Together is a step by step guidebook on helping our youth develop their best selves. Jeff Christian uses the world's #1 food to bring people together. Whether you lead a class, team, or family, this book provides tremendous insight into the power of diversity."
Jon Gordon, best selling author of The Garden and Training Camp

"It's a very easy story to read, as easy as making pizza, but with all the needed ingredients to inspire young and not so young people to change, to look at our world in a different light and to realize that together we rise."
Cristina Zenato, Education and Conservation Leader

As I read Pizza Day, "We Rise Together", I was drawn to the process of engaging today's youth that are so overwhelmed by so many forms of outside inputs. Pizza!!! Cuts through all distractions and Jeff uses it to engage and teach valuable life lessons. Children and adults can learn a lot from every slice.
Dan Weiss, Professional Basketball Player and Coach

In the story, "Pizza Day, We Rise Together," a teacher, saddened by the behavioral challenges with her new class, decides to bring her joy of cooking into her lesson plan to try and make a positive difference in the lives of her students.

Through her genuine desire to create a successful and happy environment, Mrs. Rock uses the basic fundamentals of pizza making to inspire each individual and leads them closer to building the skills necessary to live in this ever-changing world with confidence, kindness, and empathy.
Margie Harris, Mother and Psychiatric Technician

Pizza Day, We Rise Together is a heartwarming journey of a rowdy class to a band of students sharing the beauty of their true selves.
Michie Montgomery, Classified Senate Representative Area 9

Pizza Day, We Rise Together is a fun and creative story about self-reflection and the beauty of serving others. Mrs. Rock uses Pizza Day to inspire her class to look deeply within themselves, allowing them each to discover the value of respect, diversity, and love. This fun, interactive story will take you on a journey that will leave you and your children with a new perspective on friendship and community, AND leave your mouth watering for pizza! I look forward to reading this book to my own children and discussing ways we can follow in Mrs. Rock's footsteps, and the importance of taking the time to Pause, Breathe, and Smile.
Briannah Healey, Registered Nurse and future mother

Fantastic story of a group of people learning how to be a TEAM. Using PIZZA and the INGREDIENTS of Life to create a better understanding of how to be a LEADER, LISTENER, TEACHER, and TEAMMATE is a creative way of making the MESSAGE resonate. Jeff Christian has a special way of telling a story of TRUTH and INDIVIDUAL DEVELOPMENT in a family type environment!
Tom Myers, Area Scout Chicago Cubs

Pizza Day - We Rise Together has the perfect blend of likeable, relatable characters, and valuable life lessons. Teamwork, empathy, self-care and diversity are just a few of the important topics touched on in this book - all of which are valuable at any age, but are particularly impactful and important to instill in our future leaders - our children! Mrs. Rock, a dedicated and loveable third grade teacher, sees greatness in her students, even after a terrible first day of school. Through the art of pizza making, she teaches them how to value themselves and others. The included index of key words and recipes make this book fun and interactive, and one that will be read and referenced over and over again. I'd recommend Pizza Day -We Rise Together to any family or classroom of elementary school children.
Ashley Gibbs, Health Services at Sacramento City College

We Rise Together

The Pizza Day Series

by Jeff Christian
Illustrated by Kathrine Gutkovskiy

This is a work of fiction. Names, characters, places, and incidents are products of the author's imagination. Any resemblance to actual persons (living or dead), businesses, companies, events, or locales is entirely coincidental.

Text copyright © 2022 by Jeff Christian

Illustrations copyright © 2022 by Jeff Christian

Printed in the United States of America

Published by:
C4Leaders Publishing
6120 N. Vine Street
Vacaville, CA 95688

All rights reserved. No part of this publication may be reproduced, stored in a retrieval system, or transmitted in any form or by any means—for example, electronic, photocopy, recording—without the prior written permission of the publisher. The only exception is brief quotations in printed reviews.

Paperback ISBN: 9781737932024

Library of Congress Control Number: 2021919036

Dedication

Dedicated to my family for always believing in me and loving me unconditionally. We started Pizza Night and now we are sharing Pizza Day with the world. Thank you for the relentless encouragement and love.

Mrs. Rock was inspired by my mom, the one true ROCK. The image for Mrs. Rock was inspired by an amazing teacher that had a big impact on my life - Mrs. Diann Smooth.   The world is a much better place with powerful women guiding the way!

Table Of Contents

Chapter 1 Mrs. Rock 2

Chapter 2 Perseverance Wins 6

Chapter 3 The Secret Recipe 10

Chapter 4 Nurturing Ourselves 14

Chapter 5 New Opportunities 18

Chapter 6 A New Challenge 26

Chapter 7 Magic Happens 30

Chapter 8 The Tomato Sauce and Toppings . . 34

Chapter 9 Ready to Bake 38

Glossary of Terms 44

Pizza Recipe 46

CHAPTER 1

Mrs. Rock

Mrs. Rock had been teaching Third Grade at St. Lucy's Elementary School in Campbell, California for a very long time. In fact, to be precise she had taught there for 44 years.

Some of Mrs. Rock's friends would ask her, "When are you going to retire?" Mrs. Rock always had the same answer, "I LOVE my students and I have too much fun teaching and learning. I can't imagine retiring."

Every day, Mrs. Rock started class with CIRCLE TIME and a THOUGHT OF THE DAY. Her goal was to get her students to talk to one another, to truly see each other, to learn to think deeply, and to develop SELF-REFLECTION.

But when school started the next September she noticed that her class was different. The students did not want to talk to each other. They did not want to listen to one another. "Seeing" each other was not something they did and forget about learning to think deeply—they didn't have a clue on how to do that.

This group of students only wanted to make fun of each other, blame each other, and call each other very mean names.

That night after the first day of the new school year, Mrs. Rock went home and for the first time in her teaching career, she cried herself to sleep.

CHAPTER 2

Perseverance Wins

But, Mrs. Rock was not going to be down and out for long. One of her amazing qualities was her ability to PERSEVERE. Mrs. Rock might get knocked down, but she never stayed down. She was MOTIVATED to make this school year the best school year yet!

When she got up the next morning, she knew just how to make this school year one to remember!

She had an amazing idea. She was going to have a pizza day! PIZZA DAY, WE RISE TOGETHER was going to be the solution to help her students be KIND to one another! Once she thought of the idea, she got very excited about getting started on it.

Who doesn't love pizza? Mrs. Rock's idea was to teach her students how to make their very own pizza.

Mrs. Rock knew, she could use the "pizza-making" process to teach her students to listen, to trust, to appreciate differences, and to see and develop GREATNESS in each other.

She had a SECRET RECIPE to help her students. She was going to encourage them to RISE TOGETHER!

CHAPTER 3

The Secret Recipe

The SECRET RECIPE had several steps.

Step One – Feed the Starter

Sourdough pizza dough was Mrs. Rock's favorite, so she wanted to teach her students how to make the world's best dough!

"Good morning, class," Mrs. Rock began. "Today we're going to learn to make pizza dough. But, we're not going to learn to make ordinary pizza dough. We're going to learn to make sourdough pizza dough.

The students weren't paying much attention to what Mrs. Rock was saying until she said the word "pizza." They all loved pizza and started to imagine eating a slice--or more.

Once the class settled, Mrs. Rock continued, "The sourdough starter is LIVE BACTERIA that needs water, flour, and oxygen to grow and multiply. If we forget to feed the starter, the starter will die. Then the pizza-making process is over before it starts!"

One of the students blurted out, "But, Mrs. Rock, I thought bacteria was bad. Aren't we supposed to get rid of bacteria?"

Mrs. Rock smiled. "That's a great comment. There are a lot of harmful bacteria, but there are also bacteria that are very helpful. This type of bacteria is helpful. Now, I'd like you to think about something else. Do you see any connection between feeding this starter and taking care of ourselves?"

CHAPTER 4

Nurturing Ourselves

The class was quiet as they thought about Mrs. Rock's question. She waited a few minutes and then a boy in the front said, "The starter needs things to grow and we need things to grow and stay healthy too."

"Excellent!" exclaimed Mrs. Rock. "That is absolutely correct! What ingredients do we need to grow healthy and strong, both mentally and physically?"

She moved to the front of the classroom, encouraging the students to brainstorm ideas. As they did, she wrote their suggestions on the board.

"Healthy food!" one student called out.

"How about exercise?" said another.

"I think love, family, and friends are important," a shy girl in the back of the class said.

Mrs. Rock kept writing.

"A safe place to sleep, play, and live," one student said.
"How about empathy for others?" another said.
"These are all great," Mrs. Rock said.
"Books, movies, and music," said another student.
"Someone to believe in us," another student whispered.

Mrs. Rock stopped and turned to face the class. She paused at every student while she glanced around the room. "I believe in you!" she said. The students were surprised to see tears in Mrs. Rock's eyes. Then she added more words to the board. This time she expressed something that was important to her—the opportunity to serve others.

CHAPTER 5

New Opportunities

Mrs. Rock knew her students only needed the proper opportunities to ignite the greatness within them. So she provided each student with a sourdough starter, a small container, water, and flour.

During CIRCLE TIME every day, the students were asked to share how they were taking action to care for themselves and others in their lives. Just like they were doing with their sourdough starters.

Mrs. Rock's heart was full of joy during this part of class. She sat back and listened attentively. Her students' lives were changing in a positive direction right in front of her!

Houa started reading to his younger sister Suni before going to bed. They were both enjoying the stories.

Maika began playing the ukulele. His practice was making him a better musician.

Even Christian, who had been the most disruptive student in the class, shared how he was practicing his listening skills. He shared that the key to being a good listener was to _Pause_, _Breathe_, and _Smile_. Christian said that when he did, all the overwhelming thoughts in his head slowed down, and he was able to listen better.

CHAPTER 6

A New Challenge

After Mrs. Rock heard their stories, she had another CHALLENGE for her class. She told her students, that if they consistently took care of their starter, with no reminders from her, for 30 straight days, they would earn a PIZZA DAY.

Thirty days passed and Mrs. Rock's class was RISING! Alissa, all of a sudden, wanted to hold the door for her classmates.

Christian's new role was to greet every student with a smile before Circle Time. Maika asked Mrs. Rock, if he could play his ukulele for the class? Of course, Mrs. Rock said YES!!!

One day, Mrs. Rock said, "All of you are RISING! We're ready for "step two" of the SECRET RECIPE."

For "step two" we use the sourdough starter to make tasty and supportive dough. When life gets busy we should P.B.S., (Pause, Breathe, and Smile) and SLOW DOWN.

Christian has done a very good job with P.B.S., and he can help you.

Keep life simple. Simplicity is the key to making incredible pizza dough. Here is all you need:
Starter
Water
Olive Oil
Flour
Salt.

Mix the flour and salt first. Then, in a separate bowl, mix the water, starter, and olive oil. After that, combine the dry and wet ingredients and begin kneading the dough."

One day, Mrs. Rock said, "All of you are RISING! We're ready for "step two" of the SECRET RECIPE."

For "step two" we use the sourdough starter to make tasty and supportive dough. When life gets busy we should P.B.S., (Pause, Breathe, and Smile) and SLOW DOWN.

Christian has done a very good job with P.B.S., and he can help you.

Keep life simple. Simplicity is the key to making incredible pizza dough. Here is all you need:
Starter
Water
Olive Oil
Flour
Salt.

Mix the flour and salt first. Then, in a separate bowl, mix the water, starter, and olive oil. After that, combine the dry and wet ingredients and begin kneading the dough."

CHAPTER 7
Magic Happens

Mrs. Rock continued. "Something magical happens when you put your hands in the mixing bowl and you FEEL the ingredients come together to form pizza dough."

Just like the flour, salt, water, starter, and olive oil came together, so did the students in Mrs. Rock's class.

By FEEDING THEIR STARTER together, the students realized they had a RESPONSIBILITY to themselves, to their classmates, and to their teacher. It was important for them to help each other be the best they could be.

Focusing on "feeding the starter" had created a classroom culture that valued listening with empathy and trusting each other to do what you say you will do.

It also nurtured different perspectives as they became empowered future leaders.

Mrs. Rock's class was different, in the best way possible, than where they had been at the start of the school year. The class had transformed into something beautiful and they were ready for "step three."

CHAPTER 8

The Tomato Sauce and Toppings

After they had mastered the dough-making process, Mrs. Rock told them about her famous sauce, which was Step Three.

Mrs. Rock loved to garden and had a beautiful, bountiful vegetable garden. She told the students she would make her FAMOUS red sauce. It had lots of ingredients including fresh tomatoes, garlic, onions, carrots, salt, pepper, Italian seasoning, and a splash of olive oil. The students' mouths began to water listening to her describe it!

One of the students asked, "What else can we put on our pizza?"

"That's "Step Four" - "The Ingredients," Mrs. Rock said.

"Some people like pepperoni, some want sausage, some add mushrooms, some include black olives, some even put pineapple, and some just cheese."

She knew every topping or ingredient added something special to the pizza.

One of Mrs. Rock's greatest assets as a teacher was her ability to connect with each student and their unique ingredient. Her students always felt loved, respected, and empowered to become their true selves.

The students added their ingredients to their pizzas and each shared why they chose those ingredients.

Mrs. Rock was proud of each student. She knew their work in building the community would result in a world whose citizens treat ALL people with love and respect.

CHAPTER 9 Ready to Bake

"Now it's time for "Step Five." We need to "bake our pizzas" Mrs. Rock said.

The students were ready to cook their pizzas, when all of a sudden they heard a loud horn.

Outside their classroom they saw a beautiful pizza oven on the back of a truck. They were so excited!

Mrs. Rock told her students that the true magic in cooking a wood fired pizza, lies in the process: cleaning the oven floor; building the fire; getting the temperature to 700 degrees; but most importantly, enjoying each other's company while you anticipate cooking a pizza made with your own hands.

Mrs. Rock made sure her students understood the importance in "not rushing" through the process (life) and to value each step along the way.

Mrs. Rock said, "I have one last challenge for you! It's "Step Six"—"Serve Others". I want you to exchange slices of your pizza to serve your fellow students."

Her intent was to help the students realize that GIVING always feels better than receiving. Mrs. Rock wanted to teach her students about the importance of diversity-trying different things.

    Some of the students thought they may not like certain ingredients, until they tried them. The same is true for friendships. You never know who will be your closest friend until you reach out-- smile, and say hello. You might just be surprised!

    Mrs. Rock's heart was overflowing with joy because she knew Pizza Day would forever change how her students saw each other. They had all learned so much.

    She knew that the life-long lessons of empathy, trust, and diversity would empower her students for the rest of their lives.

    As they shared their pizzas, they celebrated, which was "Step Seven", time to "celebrate" their hard work. Their PIZZA DAY had turned into a Pizza Party!

Mrs. Rock arrived home later that night. She was exhausted, but elated. A huge smile covered her face when she quietly said "PIZZA DAY – WE RISE TOGETHER!" Mrs. Rock gave herself two claps, then went happily to sleep.

Glossary of Terms

Congratulations for turning to this page and find meaning to words you don't understand. When I am reading and identify a word I don't understand, I write it down on a flashcard. Then when I am done reading, I look up the definition and write it on the back of the flashcard. This process has significantly increased my vocabulary. I hope you use my idea or create one of your own. Definitions are from Merriam-Webster's online dictionary or * are Jeff's description of the word.

* **Assets** – an amazing characteristic of Mrs. Rock

Blame – to find fault with; an expression of disapproval

Bountiful – provided in abundance (i.e. many tomatoes)

Career – a job or profession for which one trains

* **Circle Time** – Mrs. Rock's way of starting class--to make sure her students felt seen and part of the class. Each student sat where they can see each other's eyes. This was very important to Mrs. Rock.

* **Diversity** – looking at the difference in people (ingredients) as a way for us to come together and appreciate each individual's unique gift.

* **Empathy** – slowing down to put yourself in a position to "feel" what another person might feel; to put yourself in their shoes without judgement.

Exhausted – extremely tired

* **Feeding the Starter** – to take action in your life; to do what is most important (eat healthy, exercise, spend time with family, read, rest…).

Knead – to press into a mass

Motivated – having a strong desire to do well or succeed

Nurturing – to encourage or to further the development

* **P.B.S. – Pause, Breathe, Smile** – a mindfulness technique taught to me by my mentor Chau Yoder. To breathe through your nose, like you are smelling a rose; then out through your mouth, like you are blowing out birthday candles; then smile (hold for 4 seconds); – repeat as necessary to feel peace/calm.

Perseverance – the quality that allows someone to continue trying to do something even though it is difficult

Retire – to conclude one's working or professional career

* **"Seeing" Each Other** – To feel, deep in your bones, that the world is bigger than you, and that you are blessed to be alive. Once you "feel" that, you can then P.B.S. to truly see your classmates; to try and listen to them and fully understand what their life looks like – without placing good or bad judgment.

* **Self-Reflection** – to take time each day, with no distractions; to sit and think about what is most important to you; what you might need help with; to think about ways in which you can grow and learn; to find peace in silence, to just listen to your heart.

* **Serve** – to give of yourself to others, with no expectation of getting anything in return, (other than your heart feeling soooooo good).

* **Thought of the Day** – a quote that Mrs. Rock used to help her students focus on what was most important for that day; to inspire, to dream, to feel hope, and know love.

Family Night Recipe

I am so excited to share the pizza making process! Time is the essential ingredient. When you decide to have your pizza night, make sure you give yourself the gift of time. Life is so busy, we are moving from thing to thing, and "family time" loses its meaning. The purpose of Pizza Night is to slow down and enjoy the process with your family. The following recipe will make seven, 240 gram (about the size of your fist), individual pizzas:

Required Supplies:
Large bowl (approximately 15 inch diameter)
1 digital scale (can use measuring cups if scale is not available)
Dough cutter (can use kitchen knife)
Pizza cutter (can use kitchen knife)

Pizza Dough
1000 grams or 8 cups unbleached Hi-Gluten flour
1 rounded tablespoon active dry yeast
20 grams or 1-1/3 tablespoons olive oil
520 grams or 1-1/8 cups cold water
2 tablespoons sea salt

Pizza Sauce
(2) 32 oz cans of crushed tomatoes
1/2 cup olive oil
1 tablespoon salt

Pizza Toppings
(2) 16 oz sliced whole milk mozzarella cheese
Toppings of your choice (no wrong answer ☺)

Other Items
(2) Pizza Stones 15 inches square (can use baking sheet)

Pizza Peel 15 inches with short handle (can use a piece of stiff cardboard)
(1) 16x12 baking sheet with cover (can use large plate and cover with plastic wrap)
Cutting board

If you would like to download the document please go to www.pizzadays.org.

Pizza Making Steps

Step 1. Pizza dough- Add flour and salt to mixing bowl. Mix with your hands to infuse the dry ingredients. In a separate measuring cup start with 100 grams of warm water (3/8 cup) and then add active dry yeast. Use a small whisk to mix yeast for about 30 seconds; dissolve yeast then mixture should have slight foam on the top. If not, check the date on your yeast package, it may be old.

Step 2. Add cold water and olive oil to the flour and salt. Mix with your hand for about 3 minutes (enjoy the ingredients slowing binding together). Next, add the warm yeast mixture and mix again for several minutes, using your hands to fold the ingredients into the center of the bowl. The dough should begin forming at this point (should feel slightly wet but you can feel the ingredients coming together). Be sure to fold in all flour from sides and bottom of bowl. Continue to fold dough into center. At this point, dough should start to look slightly shiny (you are on your way ☺). Cover dough with foil or plastic wrap; cover to let dough rest for two hours (dough should RISE).

Step 3. On a clean flat smooth surface in the kitchen, dust a small handful of flour on to countertop. Using a bowl scraper (don't have one, just use your hand) to move the dough onto the counter (sprinkle a small amount of flour on top of dough as well). You will want to use dough cutter or knife to cut dough into (7) 240 gram pieces. Currently, your dough should look pretty rough and misshapen (you have it right where you want it!).

Step 4. Proofing/balling the dough = shaping dough. *Place a small amount of flour in your hands and then pick up one of the seven pieces. Holding the dough with your hands positioned at 3 and 9 o'clock (about chest high), gently stretch the dough about two inches on each side; stretching at same time, then tuck dough under (away from your body) to center (pinching it into a ball). Rotate dough to 12 and 6 o'clock position and then move your hands back to the 3 and 9 o'clock position. *Gently stretch dough again repeat these *steps 4 or 5 times.

At this point, your dough should look smooth and slightly tight. Make sure you are folding the dough tight. After about 5 times, repeating the process, your dough should look like a circle and be ready to place (pinched side down) on a 3-inch-deep floured baking sheet. Repeat for each proof. Sprinkle flour on top of proofed dough, cover proofs and place into the refrigerator to let rest for 24 hours (called fermenting). If you are going to use dough that night, you can leave it on the counter to rise. There are lots of factors that affect the rise of your dough, temperature being the main one. If you live where it is hot indoors, your dough will rise faster, so you might want to leave it out to rise for an hour or two and then move to the refrigerator for a few hours. Take out, a few hours before you plan to use it, so the dough can be shaped (difficult to shape cold dough). Dough can over-proof as well. If you leave it out too long, it will rise too much and not maintain it's shape. Instead of eating a pizza, you will create a doughnut ☺.

Step 5. Pizza Sauce- Use a deep container (6-inch-high walls), add garlic and olive oil. Mix with a hand blender. Next, add salt, red pepper flakes (optional, we love spice), Italian seasoning, and pepper. Use the blender again to mix together. Now, add your two cans of crushed tomatoes, and mix together with a spoon. Don't use blender because it will result in watery sauce. Refrigerate for 24 hours (enhances flavors). If you are eating that night, no worries, the sauce will still be amazing!

Step 6. Pizza Night – Take sauce and dough out of refrigerator at least two hours before you plan on eating. Turn oven to 500 degrees, and place both stones in oven. (two, if possible, because toward the end of cooking the pizza, you might want the bottom of the pizza to be crispy. You need to put the pizza to a fresh stone to achieve a crispy crust).

Step 7. **Setting up Stations (Ingredients)** - Whatever you like on your pizza, set up the station to have easy access to your tasty ingredients. Once you have your stations set-up, you will then be in a ready to work on your dough (shape it). Step 8 will guide you in topping your pizza, please remember that less is more --meaning start simple, not too much sauce, not too much cheese, not too much pepperoni. The more ingredients on the pizza, the more difficult it becomes to transfer and cook. Success and happiness come from keeping your pizza and your life simple ☺.

Step 8. **Transferring Dough, Stretching Dough, Topping Dough**- First step is to flour your work surface, to ensure dough won't stick to surface. LISTEN UP - gently take your dough from the baking sheet, and gently place it on the counter (if you are rough with it, you will trigger the gluten network to bind and your dough will not stretch). If your dough (in the baking sheet) merged together, use your dough cutter (wet the edge of dough cutter) to gently separate into seven dough balls. Place one dough on the floured counter, and gently flip it over, then back again - dough should have flour on both sides. This time, add some flour on your pizza peel as well. You are ready to start shaping your dough. Start by taking your index/middle finger (side by side) and gently push (about an inch from the edge) the dough outward in a circle fashion (trying to create the shape of a pizza). This is defining the edge = your crust/rim. Next, with same technique, gently push the rest of the dough (not outer edge/rim) until it starts to get slightly wider. After doing this, gently pick up the dough, then hold the dough like you are holding a steering wheel. Gently rotate the dough around the steering wheel, being mindful to watch the middle does not stretch too much (don't want any holes). Dough should be roughly 10 inches in diameter (240 gram dough ball). Place the dough on the lightly floured pizza peel. Give the peel a little shake to make sure the dough is not sticking. If you shake and the dough doesn't move, take dough off peel and add more flour to your peel. Transfer the dough from peel to oven, so you need to make sure it doesn't stick. At this point, you need to move a little fast because the dough will get warm and

begin to stick.
Next, add your sauce (less is more) and keep it about an inch from the edge of the pizza. Next add your toppings (less is more, if you have too much, gets difficult to cook).
Give your peel a gentle shake to make sure pizza is not stuck. Assuming it is not, you will take your topped pizza to the oven (open oven and pull out rack) and place the peel (keeping it flat as possible) over the stone. Be careful, everything is very HOT. This part takes some trial and error. Lower the front of the peel so the pizza slides onto the top stone (remember you have two in the oven). Close the oven and set your timer for 5 minutes. Again, everyone has different ovens, so make adjustments as needed. After 5 minutes, get your pizza peel and slide it under the slightly cooked pizza, if it is too soft, cook it longer (you will not be able to slide peel under it). When it is slightly cooked, place the pizza on the second hot stone and set timer for another 5 minutes or so.

Step 9. Take out of oven. Place on cutting board, slice and eat. You did it! Make sure everyone has a role in your Family Pizza Night. It is not about the end product, it is really about doing something as a family, enjoying a homecooked meal together, and starting a tradition that can only get better with time. BRAVO!!!

Please reach out to me to let me know how it turned out, what adjustments you had to make, how it brought your family closer together... I would also love to see some pictures of your pizza. Please reach out to me at jeff@pizzadays.org. Thanks and take care.

About the Author

Growing up in Campbell, California as one of eight siblings, Jeff learned the value of serving others. Mostly by witnessing his mother – "The Rock," on a daily basis. *The Pizza Day Series* is inspired to share life's values through the pizza making process experience. Igniting greatness in people through storytelling is one of Jeff's focuses in writing *The Pizza Day Series*. Jeff believes in all people, and is passionate in encouraging everyone that they can overcome life's challenges. His keys to success? Take time to slow down, to truly see each other, to be seen, and listen with intention to one another.

The Pizza Day Series takes young readers, families, teachers, teams, or anyone else interested, on a journey to better themselves. Each book in the series follows an inspirational journey of communication, chemistry, consistency, and creativity (C4). The four tenets of his Non-Profit group, *C4 Leaders*. Each story will encourage the reader to "light the fuse" (take action) and implement C4 into their daily lives.

Jeff is a husband, father, registered nurse, basketball coach, podcast host of *Life's Essential Ingredients*, and is the founder of the nonprofit organization--*C4 Leaders*®. All proceeds from the sale of his books goes toward the nonprofit. *C4 Leaders*® uses pizza and pizza making to build community at no financial cost to the participants. (Although, donations are accepted and appreciated).

Grab your seat at the table and enjoy a tasty slice of homemade pizza infused with Life's Essential Ingredients!

Connect with Jeff at www.c4leaders.org or www.pizzadays.org.

Special Thanks

When I look back at my life, I will look back and see how blessed I was to have had so many people who were instrumental in helping me along my journey. Words cannot express what is in my heart—the utmost love and joy goes out to the following individuals who provided guidance in the book writing process:

Leslie and Grant Bieberdorf, Capriana Christian, Delia Christian, Donna Cowan, Milo Shammos, Tom Zipp, Renee Crevelli, Paul Mifsud, Mike Sestich, Wendy Gomez, Ashley Gibbs, Margie Harris, Ali English, Annaliese Vasquez, Kerri Mahoney, Kathrine Gutkovskiy, and Annamaria Farbizio.